Blessed Resistance

Blessed Resistance

poems by

JOAN LOGGHE

Joan Logghe

a Mariposa Book

Published by
Mariposa Printing & Publishing
922 Baca Street
Santa Fe, New Mexico 87501
505-988-5582

FIRST EDITION 1999

ISBN 0-933553-13-7
LCCN 99-70274

Acknowledgements
Some of these poems appeared in *Fish Drum Magazine, Black Bear Review,
the eleventh muse, Frank, Crosswinds, Women's Review of Books, Santa Fe Spirit
Magazine, The Santa Fe Reporter, Mothering Magazine, Puerto del Sol, Teens:
A Fresh Look (Mothering Magazine* Books, John Muir Press), *Saludas*
(Pennywhistle Press), *What Makes a Woman Beautiful* (chapbook from
Pennywhistle Press), *Poems from the Russian Room* (chapbook from
Superstitions Press), *New Mexico Poetry Renaissance*, edited by Miriam Sagan
and Sharon Niederman, (Red Crane Books), *We Speak for Peace*, edited by
Ruth Harriet Jacobs, Ph.D. (Knowledge, Ideas & Trends, Inc.), *Calendar of
Jewish Artists (*Temple Beth Shalom), *Palimpset Press Calendar , Chokecherry*
(a SOMOS Anthology), on the Internet in *Santa Fe Poetry Broadside*, Issue
#1, *Outsiders: Poems about Rebels, Exiles & Renegades*, edited by Laure-Anne
Bosselaar (Milkweed Editions), *Ride the Moon*, Vehicle: Art & Transportation
in New Mexico, *GRRRRR: Poems About Bears*, edited by C.B. Follett (Arctos
Press), and on KNME TV, *Language of Life* contest winner.

To my children, Corina, Matt, and Hope

To the community of La Puebla

✄ Contents ✄

I. SACRED GROUND

II. WHIRLWIND OF BEAUTY

III. NO CURRENCY BUT LOVE

Part One

⚜

SACRED GROUND

"I have stumbled lost and wild
onto sacred ground."

—Rosalie Sorrels

Something Like Marriage

I'm engaged to New Mexico. I've been engaged for eighteen years
I've worn its ring of rainbow set with a mica shard.
I've given my dowry already, my skin texture, my hair moisture.
I've given New Mexico my back-East manners, my eyesight,
The arches of my feet. New Mexico's a difficult fiancé.
I learned the word chamisa, and the plant takes an alias.
I plant trees for it, carry water to them. At first
New Mexico plays hard to get, says:
"Learn Spanish. Study adobe making.
Make hammered-tin light fixtures for the house."

I'm engaged to New Mexico, but I don't want to marry
New Mexico. It's too large. It burps when it drinks beer.
It leaves the toilet seat up. It likes beans cooked with lard
And chile so hot that even people born here
And nursed on a chile can't take the heat.

I tell it, "I'll date you, but I don't want to marry you."
"You promised," it whines. "It's been eighteen years."
But I was younger then. Now I'm not ready to commit.
I've been to Chicago. I've seen Manhattan
Next to a man I love. I've dined on Thai food
In Boulder, Colorado. My mother tells me,
"You could do better. New Mexico's not good enough
For you." But we're engaged. It gave me these cuticles,
These dust-devil eyes, and my Bar-None brand.
But I have to admit, even to Mom, that I don't love it anymore.
Truth to tell, it was infatuation, never should have gone on
So long. I bought rhinestones, and it threw them to the stars.
I bought velvet, and it made velvet paintings of coyotes.

I want to leave New Mexico, but it acts like it owns me.
I only wear red and black, the secret state colors. I dream
New Mexico license plates on all the cars in eternity.
It follows me everywhere like mesquite cologne,
Calls me señorita in a loud voice in public.

I love New Mexico in the dark, but I don't want its kisses,
Full of prickly pear and rattler. I want an ocean voyage.
I want a real state like Massachusetts, full of pilgrims,
Lots of grief and headlines. I want back my youth.
I'm flirting with Alaska. I've got a bad crush on Wyoming.
I'm even pining for my old love, Pennsylvania. My hope chest
Is full of turquoise and Chimayó weavings. They are all
Dusty and creased with years of waiting.

Dear New Mexico, I write. Meet me in Española
At Ranch O' Casados at 5 p.m. on Saturday. We have to talk.
It rides into Española on an Appaloosa. It carries
A lariat and ropes me in the Big Rock parking lot.
"Kiss me, darling," it drawls. Its spurs reverberate.
See what I'm up against?

Nambe Pantoum

On the Nambe road we lived three years for free.
Three railroad-car adobe rooms, heated by wood,
Water carried in, my water broke, a baby came to me.
Stork of my own two legs, beak of pain.

Three railroad-car rooms, adobe, heated by words,
Classical music of apricot trees,
Stork of my own two legs, beak of my pain.
In a Sears Roebuck rocker a baby drank me.

Classical music of cottonwood trees,
I nursed that girl all seasons through four loves
In a Sears rocker, that baby drank me.
Breasts can fill with music late in the century.

Nursed that girl all seasons through four loves,
My heart never as full of gesture as then.
Breasts can fill with music late in the century.
I rinsed her clean in a yellow plastic tub.

Never a heart as full of gesture as now.
A woman walks in beauty between two worlds.
I rinsed her holy in a yellow plastic tub,
First child, then second, so simple, love.

A woman walks in beauty between you and me.
The pilgrims passed Good Friday, nothing avant garde.
First child, then second, uncomplicated love.
I gave my hands to children, my mind to the other world.

We need the pilgrims passing, nothing avant garde.
We need the Navajo, the Spanish, and the Jews.
I gave my hands to children, my mind to the other world.
Carried a suitcase packed with candles, wine, and bread.

We need the Pueblo people, santeros carving faith.
My children are walking Sabbaths. Carve me peace out of wood.
Carry a suitcase packed with candles, wine, and bread.
My children are prayer flags, shake blessings with their breath.

My children are Sabbaths, carry me peaceful out of this world.
We carried water, my water broke, three babies came to me.
My children are prayer flags shaking blessings as they breathe.
In Nambe, like pilgrims, we lived three lifetimes free.

Española

Española before dawn is quiet
Like a lady in black lace
If you close your eyes to neon,
Lean on the remains of the gallant
Cottonwood grandfathers by the acequia,
She almost lives again in beauty.

Española before daylight unveils
Markets, gas, and burgers,
Rests like a woman in a brown cotton dress
Beside a crossing of the Rio Grande
Under a Russian olive filled with bluebirds.

Española at midday slumps
Like a housewife with a new scarf
Of turquoise rayon outside the Wash-O-Mat,
Watching traffic's thick jam
For a maroon Pontiac to drive her home
Past pigeons taking off
From parking-lot weeds.

And, if she lasts till midnight,
Española is like a teenager
In green spandex who climbs
Into the brilliant magenta gleam
Of a low rider, slides across crushed velvet,
Cruises the worn-out mile
From the Sonic Drive-In south of town
To the Sonic Drive-In north,
Buys a hamburger, and feeds magpies
Leftover french fries.

Española Pantoum

Here is a common town with 13,000 brains.
A man drives a Cadillac with a hidden gun.
A rose climbing into a woman's hair
And babies born know nothing of sin.

A man drives a Cadillac with a hidden gun.
He lectures his children, pounds the table,
And babies born know nothing of sin,
Sing to their mothers, "It will be all right."

He lectures his children, pounds the table.
Spring offers up blossoms on the altars of orchards,
Sings to the mothers, "It will be all right."
Prayers silent as whiskey hold frost away.

Spring offers up blossoms on the altars of orchards,
This land a holy ghost of faith and fruit scent,
Prayers silent as whiskey hold frost away.
A peach branch blooms pink against adobe.

This land a holy ghost of faith and fruit scent.
I want to pull over, snap like Ansel Adams
A peach branch blooming pink against a wall.
The yucca is silent, not at all spiteful.

I want to pull over, snap like Ansel Adams
The Virgin of Guadalupe on the restaurant El Paragua.
The yucca is silent, not at all spiteful.
I used to work there, got to know the families.

The Virgin of Guadalupe on the restaurant El Paragua
Will soon be covered in climbing roses.
I used to work there, got to know the families
Who live in this town and die here, flamenco.

We'll soon be covered in climbing roses.
When spring exits in a dust devil, I will miss it,
Like flamenco, those who live in this town and die here,
my camera shutter clicking its eye of castanet.

When spring exits in a dust devil, I will miss it.
Here is a common town with 13,000 brains,
My camera shutter clicking its eye of castanet,
A rose climbing into a woman's hair.

But Española

Life is sensible,
But Española with her mirror
The Río Grande and what becomes
Of wild river, and a shooting
By the new bridge, choke back
The rumors for air. Pull out
A comb from your back pocket.

You've got to get in and get out
Before eleven, before the weekend
With its steady chug,
Before you spend it all
And eat groceries from the sack,
Go home empty.

A bookstore opens and folds
Like a paperback with a torn-off cover.
But you can choose from burger stands,
Pump gas all night, forget about air.
And sometimes in the night
A truck drives in, unloads velvet couches
With flared arms of rust and gold,
Or green, and always potatoes and piñon,
Then chile, peaches, and corn.
One day melons from Pecos, Texas.
Your children beg for plaster statues
For the lawn.

This town kicks back on marijuana in the eyes
Of the guy who cleans your windshield.
A plane lands on the highway, it's dark,
Taxis with its lights off
Three miles out and you always wonder.
Later on, farther out on the edge
Of town a ball of fire rolls.
You know what that means.

But Friday I pull the plug
And the Río gurgles away
Sucking the town with it, the fields too,
Each down their acequia from the source,
The apple orchards north,
And all you smell is earth.

Return to Española

I was gone two days.
When I got back, my children had aged,
My husband's beard grown in for winter.
Everyone was driving around town
Taking a bite out of a golden delicious.

Pumpkins on the stands
And the air was all chiles roasting,
A smell so meaty, romantic, immediate
That I know it is the soul of this valley.

The apple is the heart and the sex
Is the cars, sleek and personal
With fur dark interiors.
They are so private
I don't want to talk about it.
And then they stop, mid-road,
Grown suddenly gregarious,
News shouted between open windows.

I forgot to mention the brain.
The brain is not neon,
But the fingers of old ones
Who know without telling.
They tamp the roots of new peach trees,
Say rosaries.

When I leave I think
Leaving is where my art lies,
Cooler towns with less business.
My norths, my nights awake
Where I retreat to flatter my life,
Feed her a rich, imported diet.

It's not like returning to a city
Where the air lead-pipes you,
Where you crawl up to your apartment
And don't know if you're home.
Coming back in like whitewalls and new rims,
To a town where I get flats fixed,
Curse traffic, pray my way home.

The man I saw first was the butcher.
His sausage sculpted into a hog,
Poked eyes, pinched ears, nose
Flat against the glass. Our mom-and-pop
Grocery, rare these days
As our mom-and-pop family,
As cottonwood leaves in November,
Purple low riders and soul.

La Puebla

Place endangered by beauty, too good
For its own good. A pharmacopoeia
Of sand hills and housing, dirt
Roads and tense vistas. She lives here.

She came here crying, "Que viva!" her past
A sad fist relaxing. She stayed, sanctified by place.
Her bedposts in four directions make prayers
Around the archipelago of dreams.

Her family drones through squadrons of duties,
Drives in and out bumbling over the washboard roads
To rendezvous with money.
Who holds the open till?

This immaculate place is elemental
Stillness. Quiet as inheritance.
She adorns the day with food and music.
The immaculate sky is the jazz they sleep under.

She blasts through boredom to a strategy
For loving. The clouds aggrandize the horizon,
Mansions of cliff hold dens for coyote.
Cliché cannot abide in these vistas.

This small place with its dusty fandango,
Will you buy everything? Will you sell?
Real estate of sleeping, we wake up
Sabotaged and taxed.

We wake up like Pharaoh's wrapped body.
We wake up too small, shrunken by heat
And subdivision. We wake up verbose
And on fire. In La Puebla,

Little scenic saint of a place. Years deepen.
The alarm, the riverbed, the invented, the holy,
The sold, the purchased, the lost orchards,
The last fictive homeland.

Stolen Landscape

We bought the land, clear title,
purchased acreage you cannot own,
Got a deed, made monthly payments
On the mourning dove.

We own the wheeling of ravens
And the aquifer. We drilled 200 feet,
A well that is inalienably ours.
We buried wires, the lithography of charge.

We bought land with our Vibram soles
And our celestial heads. With our
Gregorian hearts and our singing wallets
We built cathedrals: the house,
The chicken coop, the barn.

We were always thirsty, we bought
windows. We had children here.
They each came out wrapped in mylar
With their fresh karma and eyelashes,
Their disco throats and lanolin skin.

We bought six acres in the old days,
Which were not any better than now.
These are the good days, before flood
And after drought. Floozy arroyo
And incontinent sky. We swivel from past

To future. Walking this land, we wear bracelets
On our ankles and take sabbaticals.
We dab scent on our pulses and sit
On serapes. The cacophony of running
Commentary, the scintillating magpies.

We invite saints for dinner. Sinners arrive.
We do not dress for tea or have guests
For the weekend. The catastrophe is ours.
We do not wait for the Second Coming.
The new millennium washes our dishes

On this unpredictable land, a palette filled
With Russian olives and views
That are ours. That we paid for.

Finally Present

Praying to the Virgin again today
I made matzoh ball soup that sang.
It was the kind of singing soup we make
In New Mexico, pungent with past, lyrical,
Hidden, flecked with Catholicism.

I stood inhaling the landscape
My children first sniffed when they came out
Onto this planet of beauty and bureaucrats,
Sorrow and barrancas.

Today there was loving and failure.
There was sighing that came, not down.
From the sky as usual, or sideways from winds
And crosscurrents of angels, but up
From the earth full of blood.
Up from the diligent earth that turns
Everything back into time.

I love the sweet earth. I will stay
With my husband forever, I know
Who I love and what I ache for. Man
And mountains. Children and toads that sing at first rain.
We share each other with landscape.
The sighing and singing are kin.

My daughter slept in the car at the end
Of a meeting. I was being perfect in public and failing
What matters. Amazing that life is such
Cherries and stones. We silently age,
Fasten our fruits to the harvest, land
On the land where we planted ourselves.

I welcome myself into town. Thank the old-timers
For handsome faces and houses roofed with God.
I never sleep without their air in my heart,
Having just arrived from Pittsburgh,
With my past on my back weighing 20 years.
I am finally present in the West.
It has taken this long to catch up with the beauty.

Driving North

We stopped in Hernandez for as many
Bing cherries as would fit in a paper sack.
Driving north, pulled by a longing for Colorado,
An alpine cool.

I followed in my guidebook the geology:
"The rift of Río Grande, Permia, Triassic,
the El Rito formations lie unconformably
across eroded older rocks."

But I don't want the names of strata.
I want the way my feet hang in water off a boat,
The way long love grows down long, through
Water grasses, sediment, grows headlong down.

Facts swim through my mind.
Thought grows slick, fast, like the crowded
Trout at Red River hatchery, silver ribbon
Of solid fish force-fed in concrete vats.

I want in the best words what women know.
Not the named earth, not the hatchery trouts'
Hurried amazement but smooth release into wild river.
A moment oblivious to the man in hip-boots.

I eat as many cherries as I want.
It's exorbitant to be alive.
I can't afford to miss any of it.

Marriage of Heaven and Hell in Española

"Arise and drink your bliss for everything that lives is holy."
—WILLIAM BLAKE

"Española is built over hell."
—ANONYMOUS LOCAL WOMAN

The summer with its tint
Of heat. Mountains have never been breasts
Except when I'm alone. Except at sunset
When color makes cleavage.
We drive to town, stop at Blake's
Lotaburger. You order with, I without onion,

Hopeful for kisses, I pointedly avoid onion,
Though we may or may not collide, tint
Each other with sex. Read William Blake's
"Marriage of Heaven and Hell," his excess of breast,
And of brain. We may not cleave
Man to woman, our vague bodies absent as sunset.

I love this small town at sunset.
I come out from buying bread and onions,
Eastern sky reflects maximal color, cleavage
Of night from day, last-chance tint
Of a moment. We all have breasts
For hearts to hide out in. Even at Blake's

The man ordering for his family, at Blake's
By the Plaza, main street center of sunset.
Extra glance at the server, all breasts
Were made for admiration. Hold the onion,
That man with king cab truck, sunglasses tinted
Dark as pickup windows. Her cleavage

His salvation after a workday. The cleavage
Of gems is even, sharp between work and leisure. Blake
Would agree with us about passion. The tint
Of emotion is deep in a town. Sunset
Is main event, the day like an onion
We chop through and weep into. Men hum to the breast

Of their women on cool Friday evenings. Breasts
Are not magazine perfect. Hidden eggs perfect cleavage
In sacred mitosis, babies grow like pearl onions.
We're private as Blake's
Wife reading by the fire at sunset
Where he gazed and envisioned. Totally tinted

By God, seeing angels with breasts, old man Blake
One who shunned cleavage between God and sunset,
Sunflower and onion, passion and its daily tint.

Summer Mysteries

Grasshoppers the size of clocks. Grasshoppers
Riding lizards and playing handball.
Grasshoppers the size of mangoes gobbling starlings.

Starlings are shot for robbing the bluebird's
Nest. Starlings are dropping down chimneys
Playing violins in the hearths. In the holiest
Churchyard a young girl with her grandfather's gun
Popping birds like iridescent popcorn into death's mouth.

Young girls the size of old Oldsmobiles. Young
Girls riding horses and playing hopscotch on
The roofs of prisons. Young girls with hair
Like skylooms dreaming of their mates who are
Red sunsets on feet transplanted from Cuba.

Sunsets the size of spaniels. Sunsets riding
The Jemez Mountains and playing harpsichord.
Sunsets with roses in their hair and vacuous
Expressions, yearning for another lifetime,
A festival of death and rebirth in their teeth

Like Kama Sutras for enhancing the pleasure
Of naked moments. Stunning the starlings,
Causing them to drop, their bellies full
Of grasshoppers, out of the night sky, down
The chimneys of young girls, soot for centuries.

Waxing New Mexican

La Puebla is beautiful in the fall.
It is like Paris in the spring
Without the baguettes, and without
The boulevards. It is exactly like
Paris, only there are no sycamores
And no Maurice Chevalier. Exactly
Like Paris with cottonwoods and
A small river named Santa Cruz.
Like Paris without the Seine,
Without Le Moulin Rouge, Montmartre,
Or, "comment ca va?"

La Puebla is glorious, all yellow
With death and exactly like Paris,
So I know the poets soon will be arriving.
To one who said, "Anyplace can be
Paris," I am writing you from my Paris,
In the foothills of the Sangre de Cristos,
In the valley of lost French souls,
Paul Verlaine and Baudelaire.
The lavender fields of southern France
Send decorous odor such a long way
To my Cowboys-and-Indians West.

Land Grant

I would never raise a child in Española,
Except I've raised three, five miles out on the lip
Of the Río Grande, a slash of cool singing,
The metacarpal of the valley. This valle borracho,
This stupid valley, licked by piñons
That blast me with vigor and color.
This old place, violent and home.

Roan horses, aperitif of sunrise, ardent hollows
Of silence where my house is. I gave birth
To three, adding to the thousands who abound here,
Grow carrots and older, grow chile and wiser.
Fall out of apple trees, fallout of Los Alamos,
The Alleluia of bombs and then its bane,
Evil as old as Cain.

The liqueur of sunset, my children poised
For Christmas photos against a butte
And a mesa, against Sangre de Cristos
Hallowed by leaf loss and snow, by sunset
Smattering the western slopes with blood.
Succinct this life of ours, a mishmash of awe
And decrepitude, a span of vista and exhalation.

Why bother to die? Why not go on living in the
Valley, like a lady wearing gloves, a lady
Of zeal and masculinity, like a man effeminate
With wonder? We lie down and rise up in Spanish.
We are educated by the eminent. No school like WOW!
No education as fine as the chemistry of life force.
Opulent, our lives, quietly channeled like canyons.

My children live with vision. We wake them to eclipse
And planets. They dream through coyotes and dogs.
Look, there is a double rainbow. They barely rise
From their chairs as they are seated in beauty;
Its extravagance has no fingers in them. Look,
We say, having given them what we assume is loving.
They finger electronic toys, entranced and vivid.

Their bodies contain hollows that replicate what is
Río Grande, curves duplicate Jemez. We adults
Are bastards to this terrain. They are native.
They do not strain at Spanish. Have ingested place
Where ancient mammals walked. Taken for granted.
Given as birthright, this holy glittering world.

Visions and Ristras

We stop at the first place. Same face as last year.
Cowboy hat. Gray moustache. A vaquero. A dude.
Shakes my daughter's hand, my husband's, mine.
From this man born in Mora, we got a scrawny tree,
Last year, waiting till late. I boycott piñon,
My politics won't allow this slow grower, nut
Yielder, though the cutting's already done.

Today, biggest tree we ever got, a fir,
Branches spread and fine, perfect top for angel,
Full bottom, sold. He tells my daughter to be good,
"Be good to your mom and dad." He has fourteen
Of his own, and twenty grandchildren. He knows,
Has been around. Lives these weeks before the holidays
In a camper shell right on Riverside, the road back north.

Of all festivities, this one makes my husband smile.
To buy a tree, a sacred bargain for our life,
Ten dollars, a cheap secret. Española is cool.
Old people abound, carrying the past
On their faces. Carrying some wisdom
On their palms, psalms under their hats.
I love the winter with live nativity scene

Each Christmas Eve, bonfire and Virgin, donkey
And lamb, and bowls of posole, biscochitos,
Inside the flower shop. Six months from summer where
The woman named Betty at the feed store

Owned by the mayor sells baby chicks, ducks,
And feed by sacks loaded by my friend
With the bad back. As teenage boys trap
My daughter's eyes, visions and ristras catch mine.

Christmas Day I'll go to dances at Santa Clara or
San Juan. What could be better, the built-
In deaths and the ceremonies of innocence?
Biblical and harsh in this valley, the wild
River passes. Stores close more than open,
A bookstore finally takes root, and angels
Love the sinners. I own the air; God owns the water.
The children own the future, and my husband,

Part saint and part illusion, commits his life
To loving and to working. Black leather jacket
On a baby, bottle of Coke at the burnt-down Wash-O-Mat.
Twenty years passed through me, birthing and yearning,
Burning my bridges. Settled in the valley,
Five miles out, in the foothills where cedar catches
Its breath, and ridges of horse trails beckon,
I barely move. Buddha makes house calls.

God inhabits the mountains called Sangre de
Cristos. Right at sunset, best view of eternity.
The infinite is pink and ephemeral. It turns out.
My house never holds a cleaning; the sky can't hold
A color down. We wash by. Land is a painted moment,
And the man shakes my hand, wishes us more
Than we bargained for, buying a tree on the holy solstice,
In the center of known and unknown worlds.

New Mexican Angels

New Mexico's the place the angels go
When they retire. They like the climate.
Craving high altitudes, they lift off altars
Of ancient churches to swoop on wings
Of flaking paint.

Women call out, "Holy!" in the afternoon,
Test light between fingers to see if it's done.
There's a powdery residue, the fallout of God.
Angels settle on red rooftops to sun,
Sit on the hood of the shiniest cars,

Wave at waitresses in fast-food establishments,
A parade of blessings that nobody sees
Except a few old ones who are tuned
Beyond cash-and-carry
To the frequency of angel.

Fabric on girls' bodies fits close.
The man at the drive-in liquor store leans out
To see who's coming, thinks, "Spirits,"
But it's angels, heard in scraps of Spanish music
That waft from cars.

They can't get enough of love and sorrow,
It spills out onto the town.
They long for Spain before the Inquisition
With vague memories of faint balconies,
Women throwing gardenias and bay leaves.

New Mexican angels sigh. The wind whips up
A little and they joust dust devils
For air supremacy. Armed with fragrance,
They always win. They lift through apple
About to bloom, and cherry.

That's why the fruit blooms too soon
In Velarde, and all along the river.

Christ in the Desert Monastery

Where the Chama river pulses, the solid sky
And the earth are lined with Abiquiu
Red rock. We drive west with a lotus
In our hearts. We're not about to flirt
With random crows, errant rabbits, highway clues.
My daughter, Hope, is among our number.

We arrive at stillness, mistake the number
Of clouds for prayers. We scan the sky
And hope blue holds. We have no clue
About time. Its flat hand releases us from Abiquiu.
Winter of no snow, now death only flirts
With me, and Buddha calls from full lotus.

Ordinary day unfolds like an origami lotus.
We happen to be visiting in number.
We fan out, walk alone. Silence flirts
With our mouths. I'm as still as possible with sky
Above as ballast. I've left my coherence in Abiquiu.
My daughter is impressed by silence. It's a clue

To loving her. Words often break us down. Clue
To any love, allow emptiness to grow the lotus.
I found the Virgin again, facing Abiquiu.
Her glance beats my heart back from the numb.
My daughter and a dog share lunch with the sky.
Old tumorous Weimaraner sniffs the river, flirts

With us until the bell rings. The river flirts
By. We wander to the chapel to find clues
To God that monks hold. Out domed windows, sky
Is met by cliff. Incense is fragrant as lotus.
We watch men enter in blue tunics, wait for number
Of the psalm. "None for Ordinary Time." There's no Abiquiu.

I live a short way south of here, past Abiquiu.
This is one place I cannot even flirt
With living, being a woman and a Jew. I number
The men now praying. Do you have any clue
How monks can live in chastity, lotus
Of their sex turned back to God? The sky

Is the lover of Abiquiu. We scan sacred text for clues
On how to answer when the body flirts. Hedonist lotus
Of desire, the number of illusions is endless as sky.

Her First Jew

For Sunny Dooley

We walked the track by the Branch College,
One mile, then two, then crescent moon.
That story about her life, why she got old
In the stretch of youth called gather-me-to-you
I won't repeat because it's hers to tell.
The dark fell out of the east.
I was her first Jew. She told me in the safe space
Between public bathroom stalls.

We ate at Jerry's on Coal Avenue, a place Navajos go.
She was my first Navajo if you count a sit-down
Meal, sacramental burritos, and I do.
I liked that she drove to Española, four hours,
For Coke in bottles. That's where you find it,
She told her niece. We both know the way
Coke tastes on a hot day over the lip of green,
Polished like sea glass from prying off caps.

The snow falls sideways in Gallup,
Like an old woman sweeping out the corner
Of the sky. I feel like I might never leave.
My car could break down, my family lose my number,
And I'd live here, above Red Mesa Art Center
With its show about women, until I'm given
A new name, wearing my white shell earrings:

"First Jew Who Took Root." My gray hair
Might fall from my head and I'd grow young here
Next to the library. My plaster heart would crack
Revealing a silver heart, inside that
A heart of rose quartz, and finally the small
Passion heart beating pearls of blood.

She said right away, "I think Navajos and Jews
Have a lot in common." I was so astonished
I never asked her what, because she said
I was her first Jew, though she's met us before,
A tribe more hidden than chosen. For her
I would be wise and perfect, a female emblem
Standing for what's best in my people.

But she's no fool, knows humans
Are not perfect, not even Moses.
We are the people; God is God and carries
Perfection for us on the platter of the sky.
We share a meal and talk, to each
Other and into a larger listening.

Insomnia Litany

I am a Jew among sunflowers, a Jew
Among stars. I am a Jew with allergies
In the night, with a voice like pollen.
I am a Jew among tortillas and refried
Beans, a Jew among Virgin of Guadalupe
Candles. It took fourteen to just survive
The winter. I am a Jew among crosses,
Even the compass on the dash makes
A statement of sorts. I am a Jew
Among bankers and grocery clerks.

I wear clothes like a Jew does.
I eat foods a Jew eats. I pay bills
Like a Jew, and like a Jew I lie down,
Thanking and worrying, praising and sighing.
All my days I will be a Jew, and my nights,
Among other definitions of myself.
I will chew like a Jew. I will purchase
Stamps in rural post offices. When the man
Says, "I jewed 'em down," I will pleasantly say,
"Be careful. You never know who you're talking to.
I am a Jew." I will walk back to my car
Like a Jew, feeling the strain of having
To speak my peace among strangers
In line at Santa Cruz.

I find my way back to the old ladies
From Europe, schlepping their groceries
Home in a sack. I make jokes like a Jew.
Then my husband who loves me like a Jew
Loves, belying my mother's weekly speech
That Jewish men make the best husbands,
Wraps around me and holds me like a human.
And I love him and sleep most humanely,
All night engraved in a landscape of ghosts,
The *oy, oy, oy* of love. I sleep the sleep
Of the unlabeled. An uncircumcised sleep.

Tashlich at Embudo Crossing

*"This is the day the world is conceived. On this day
all living creatures stand up for discernment."*
—RABBI CHAVAH CARP

I yell, "Negativity!" fling bread
Into the Río Grande, Rosh Hashana
This year, 5757, year of drought, loss,
Too many young deaths. Rare rainy

Afternoon, three menopausal women
Scanning our bodies, our tapped hearts
For what has missed the mark.
We call them sins. Turn from each other

Searching our core. "Lust, greed.
Lack of discipline!" Flag of my ego, shards
Of braided bread. "Passivity, hard-heartedness."
We scour our crannies for crumbs, throw

Sin into forgiving current. Downstream
Three strangers shoot a roll of film,
Capturing while we, for now, release.
The Río Grande always was a prayer.

The river washes, washes, a giant tear.
Picture Moses lifted. Picture the Sea
Of Reeds, all that water has been made to bear.
Teshuvah means turn inward.

Ask for inscription in a holy year.
Lately, the years hold lessons we've come
To fear. We dip apples in honey for sweetness,
Ask to be inscribed in the Book of Life.

We fling the last piece in silence, naming
To ourselves what we won't frame
In the chosen air. We hold back
Nothing from the river. Emptier, we leave,

Drive south. Good medicine of river. God
Who knows about turning
Noise into silence, air into bird, water into fish,
Takes these morsels and makes a river in us.

Troubadour for Peace

Across the valley, in my line of vision,
Los Alamos, quantum leap into plutonium.
Spring arrives windy and fragrant.
Water crests, rafters float the Río Grande.
Like winter, idealism is gone.
My husband on his mare urges with knees, gallops.

I watch him ride off at a gallop.
So familiar, sweet romance of vision,
The whole blurred world a fake, reality gone
To industries of war. Scant breeze between me and plutonium.
The river's on fire at sunset, the Río Grande
Rinses air clean. My house is fragrant

With dinner. My children arrive, fragrant
Because they are mine. Off I gallop.
If I run, I may last longer. The Río Grande
Inside me is just blood, but with new vision
Of long life, grandchildren under the trees.
Plutonium is not in this picture. Be gone,

War and men making bombs. Be gone,
Lovers of money and flame. False as fame and fragrant
As deception are the men who feed plutonium,
Convince themselves it's moral, like cowboys who gallop
Off to lynch and hang. This is archaic vision.
Even I with strong glasses see past this illusory río.

Plutonium Grande will not stop at the río,
But drift downstream where I'll be writing till I'm gone.
I am entitled to life with visions.
I see Los Alamos not as it is, but old fragrant
Canyons and mesas. Peace from here to Gallup.
Defense plant, turn in your tuxedos of plutonium.

I've got to get off this trip about plutonium!
It runs me like rafters run the Río Grande.
Better a lullaby. Cowboy songs to gallop
Us to sleep. We're here today, I sing it gone,
Gone to the heaven for old bombs, herded by fragrant
Cowgirls, backlit by sky, out of our vision.

Better a vision
Without the shadow of plutonium.
Not Pluto's path, but fragrant
Days, picnics by the río
With the war god gone.
Life doesn't crawl by, it gallops.

Alone in April

Rain in New Mexico brings ulterior blessings.
Not only moisture, but leisure. Like a farmer
Who can't plant today, I have to abandon
My plan for my body, a brisk walk to the dam,
A chat with a friend about her pending divorce.

A forced solitude I require like lime
In posole. I don't know the reason but
I know the need. It's gotten Hawaiian or Indonesian,
A place where rain is native. I grow Chinese
And interior. Porcelain has dust. Plates

Piled on the drainer. My white horse could
Have been named Onion, but we called him White
In our alternative language. The fridge is full
Of dyed Easter eggs, mildly decorative. So much
I do not understand about this domestic stance.

We live too far to walk, too dry to swim.
What we call town has wildly high real estate.
The view we moved here for is filled with roofs
And burning trash in barrels. Landmark
Of satellite disk instead of Truchas Peaks.

I am alone, though my son is on computer.
The radio has Tess Gallagher's voice on low.
It's turned to snow. Tess is climbing in bed
Next to one she loved who went to landscape.
My son wears long-john bottoms and no top.

Next year he's gone, two out the door, one
Still swinging on it, nine times at nine. Alone
Is where the heart is. God gave me many Sabbaths.
I celebrate them all. Drive nowhere.
Dry land woman, regional heart.

Part Two

WHIRLWIND OF BEAUTY

A whirlwind of beauty
Passes through the eye of a needle.
A grizzled man in a blue
Checkered shirt leans in
At your front door, says,
"Sons, too, come and pass.
A whirlwind of beauty."

Annunciation

—For Gioia Timpanelli

When she walked into the angel
Both nostrils open
Quivering like the live nose
Of a deer,
How did it smell?

Like incense that is a mix of trees,
Cinnamon, cedar, and pine.
Or like water at the edge
Of a pond where spiders skid
And the eggs of frogs in ribbons
Chromosome and prayer beads
Generate their own tadpoles.

How was her belly,
Her most vulnerable?
The underside of porcupine.
The trust of a small animal that sleeps
All four legs stretched up.
The frog's white underbelly,
Thin of skin and moist.
I know she had not eaten,
Not fasted.
Her thoughts were elsewhere,
Graceful as snowdrifts.

She envisioned a golden egg
With a royal blue yolk.
Her mind hovered
Hummingbird and moon.
Idea grew flimsier and fine.
She was translucent in three places
And smelled of angel.
You could see through.

Surrender

I took off my watch
When labor began.
For weeks there was only
Time of cries and breezes
Only the time of iris
Bloom.

The day was spring
And so was the hour.
The minute was milk
And the feeling.
Days turned over
And over, like a chorus
Of lull, hush, and swaddle.
Pins fastening, unfastening
And slow closing
Of fontanels.

I was in love with fists
And knuckles.
It was surrender
As total as a country
Under white flags
Taken over by
Legions of peace.

Piercing

Summer solstice on the king-size bed
Her eyelids flutter, slit open, close into sleep.

Next to her father, her breath
Is the huff of the yogi before bliss.

In her coral bracelet to ward off
Ojo Malo, she is breathing in summer.

Should we get her ears pierced,
Tiny gold balls in her lobes?

The grandmother says, *No!*
It's barbarian.

We'll wait six summers or so
Until she asks, begs.

Until she can brave the pain
And lick down soothing ice cream,

Initiate in the shopping mall
Where piercing begins.

At a Wedding

My baby and I take a moon bath.
A strange man holds her. He wears
An Our Lady of the Rockies T-shirt.

The air of Santa Fe cools, and mountains
Sink into night, featureless
As her face before it was born.

Weeks ago, I opened up,
Was big enough for day and night,
The wedding and the honeymoon.

She breathes cool air in, warms it,
Breathes out. My face catches her scent.
She's my incense, rose that opens daily.

She is my background music.
Her hands curl, sweet mudra
Of youth. This marriage is true.

I bask in her breath, moon bath.
I can feel light fingers. I know how
Our Lady of the Rockies loved that touch.

Catalpa

Outside the back door is new sod.
We planted green, by love and money,
And the yellow sprinkler swirls it alive.
My daughter in a pink swimsuit runs
Back into the chill of sprinkler,

Squealing as if her childhood
Is the happiest place on American earth.
The clothesline hangs low, weighted
By garments of five people,
By love and green, green money.

Sheets droop and wind through lacey underwear,
White boxer shorts drying from the bottom up,
Damp just under the clothespins.
The cliffs beyond the barrancas lit pink.
Our Japanese pine grows a foot a year.

And two miles down the road, a catalpa tree
I will never see is flowering,
Domestic orchids under fat fan leaves.
I love the catalpa more than what I see.
It's what I can't see that I always love.

Between Features

Tonight at the Starlighter Drive-In, next
To Red's Steak House, next to the blinking radio tower,
We take our small daughter. Last weekend before school,
Stay out late, eat Milk Duds, popcorn. Summer
Is practically gone. It went fast. It went slowly.

The Opera down the highway is playing La Bohème.
I missed it. Lightning, on-and-off rain, the sunset
Frozen and peculiar. My hand on your chin. The girl
Sits between us, doses off. Used to be your hands
Were the voices of tenors.

"Who Wrote the Book of Love" on the radio. Perfect
For a night like this. Cars full of families, teenagers
Dance next to a camper between features.
Three times the preview sticks and celluloid burns.
We love an artificial moment, laugh knowingly.

"Española," we say. We coddle each other. Next movie
Our child sprawls asleep, pillows from home under
A meteor shower. We are natural, protect the volume
Of love. Movie lines in our mouths. Fall into a life,
A set, into a family. Write the book in a green pickup.

Art and Teenagers

Raising teenagers has its own surrealism.
Inside a woman's body in designer jeans
Is the baby you rocked, an automobile
Shifting from first gear to moonscape.
She soars, her arms cocked as in Burmese dance.
Clocks melt at curfew hour, torsos disconnect.
As if in dream, she enters the house.

"The truth is no longer certain," she says,
"Teenagers have to tell lies. "
It's trompe l'oeil. Midnight drives by
Down Route 66, the sixties revisited
By flower children's children. And drugs,
The specter in psychedelic posters
Lit by black light.

In conversation we are cubist and minimalist,
What is square and what is unsaid.
I could be a better mother, I think,
But that's romanticism, rich in pigment
But dated. Too thick,
I slather on coats of oily love,
While talking to teens is high cool.

By now it's pop art comics, op art mazes.
You know they know you don't understand,
Ought to try a new form, something Japanese,
Three strokes, less said.
You hand her a dishtowel, allowance,
You glance at her laundry once.
But then it softens, you drop the technique.

There's the person you are, flawed
And perfectly human, standing
On your own piece of vinyl flooring,
No wax, low gloss, and the person she is,
Ancient art: two women facing the same direction,
Egyptian water urn, Etruscan temple wall,
A bolt of fabric.

High School Graduation Pantoum

The dark boy leans against his pickup truck.
His heart widened into Romeo when he met my daughter.
I say to myself, "It's not worth creating a tragedy."
With the Blood Mountains behind them for Verona.

His heart widened into Romeo when he met my daughter,
A girl pulling him by the arms down the driveway
With the Blood Mountains behind them for Verona,
The wild plum blooming, they will make sour fruit.

A girl pulling him by the arms down the driveway,
Not long ago, her arms reached, her face ached red for me.
The wild plum blooming, it will make sour fruit.
Passions so sweet, grape couldn't turn wine without it.

Not long ago her arms reached, her face ached red for me,
Crying through playpen bars as I gardened,
Passion so sweet, grape couldn't turn wine without it.
I thinned lettuce, her stomach full of milk and need.

Crying through playpen bars as I garden,
Time is a rascal magpie pecking at the corn.
I thinned lettuce, her stomach full of absence.
I sat next to her yelling, "Brakes!"

Time is a rascal magpie, exotic in the corn.
A yogi asked, "What if this baby should die?"
I sit next to her driving, yelling, "Brakes!"
My heart beats audibly past midnight curfew.

A yogi asked, "What if this baby should die?
Her tongue is long." He wrote on his slate at Lama Mountain.
My heart beats audibly past midnight curfew.
At Christ in the Desert I cried in the chapel for loss.

Her tongue is long, he wrote on his slate in silence.
She's kissed a boy she loved and some she didn't.
At Christ in the Desert I cried in the chapel for loss.
I sat with older mothers who had moved on.

She's kissed a boy she loved and some she didn't.
The dark boy leans against his pickup truck.
I sit with older mothers who have moved on.
I say to myself, "Let go. It's not worth creating a tragedy."

A Giant Beauty

The daughter becomes a woman. I'm mourning
The cut ribbon announcing the launch of the ship.
I spend her like a golden egg at market, take
Home the basket, empty, singing.

I plant the magic beans and grow a giant beauty.
And then, with my masculine hands, I must chop
The vine and grow inside myself the Tree of Life.
Sending the children off, the commerce of this story.

Back to the basic blessings. Bread, a few grapes,
The color of eggplant in the clouds. My heart
Crackles like cellophane. Space, space. I write her
Free. Hand her her Gretel papers. Send her

On horseback by moonlight. Send her to ovens
And to sweetness, to distances and wiles.
My daughter becomes a woman in a painting
On someone else's wall.

Quatrains for Corina

Retablo of the Virgin on the mantel
By the green votive candle. You painted
Retablos over Christmas. The candle
Burns so I might win a prize.

I dreamed I lost and the deadline passed.
I will not win the prize, but I have you,
Firstborn, woman at college in the north.
I did not win the prize. Your eyes

Looked me mother and mother. I braided
My dark hair into your blond, arranged
For the days to go right in you. Let you go
North with its landscape of avalanche.

Sad as the empty church, I still gave you
Your almost May Day birth and your name
From a May Day poem in my college text.
Your brother came, short labor. You said, "Nice head."

Your sister came so late none of us thought
Our family could fit more love. Good Fridays
Came with pilgrimage. Passover with its sedar plate.
A lamb shank roasted with an egg.

Sweet kosher wine to dip for Egypt's plagues.
My life is biblical as the parting Sea of Reeds,
As armies dipped in wine, as blood over doors.
As Moses' miraculous snake, tablets carved by God.

I still have all of you and a man of bone.
I capture summer peaches in jars,
The root cellar to cool the sweetness down,
Laundry that multiplies, candles that burn.

I may not win another chance at life. I may
Have just this January as abode. The Virgin
In my belly calls your name. Corina,
When you gazed, you lit the mother flame.

I have no Pulitzer, or Nobel Prize, nor am I
Likely to be a household name. Not lottery,
Sweepstake's glance or green race to fame.
I may not win a prize, but I cannot lose.

God walked out of me in you, in Red Goose
Shoes. You make beauty around you like
A Navajo. I may not reach samadhi this go round,
But I love exquisitely and I let you go.

Daughter At College

Daughter with your teeth in Colorado
And your voice on the telephone.
Daughter who came first and in a hospital,
Carrying my father in her pores.
Daughter who sat in cold mountain runoff
From Truchas Peaks, laughing, throwing rocks.
Daughter who threw crayons in tantrums,
Who hated her brother, told him bad words.
Daughter who storms into my life carrying clothes
In a duffel, books falling from her arms.
Daughter who sends Easter candies and bunnies
That dispense Pez to other daughter, forming
A watershed of sweetness. Daughter of sugar,
Daughter of piney distance, of early sex
And beautiful laid-back boyfriends. Daughter
Who tells me, get down on the floor and play.
Daughter with a mind that runs counterclockwise.
Daughter with flea market bargains taking up lifetimes,
Buying her own clothing and flunking Geology.
Daughter of cloud. Daughter learning winter, so much snow
She almost drowns in college. Pine needles, black dog,
Blond boy in dreadlocks. Saying the word, *totally*,
Totally often. Daughter of collect calls, out of earshot,
Who read Italian Folktales by Italo Calvino, 700 pages,
While daydreaming through third grade. Odd beauty.
Her Grandma Leona's bones, knowing how to clean in Swiss.
Her Grandma Beti's eyes, loving in Hungarian. Most beautiful
First child of my first life. Only child in a family
Of three only children. Sent to me for painful gestures of love.
You shop your way toward knowledge. Pass a hat

To collect wisdom. Lottery daughter. Fast-food
Daughter. No car of your own. Between cities,
Seattle and Miami, there in one locale.
I call it daughter.

Outside Pagosa Springs

1.
It was the bear with a talent
For slow grazing that hit against
My daughter's car, Red Subaru
With the Pleiades on the hood.
The young female bear
Lumbered out of dark
Into a beam of light and back
Into dark again. The bullet
From the State Police stanched
Her pain. It was my daughter
Driving north for love. In our
Family we always head that way—
Into the bear, due north, in fur.
It was the thud of bear my girl
Age twenty knew. Same year
She stopped eating meat, her
Senses grew too keen. She bought
Cranberries, rose hips, honey
At the store. The light grew strange
And thin on her. When she was young,
Her beastly beauty proved too much
For me. I wished for ancient Greece
Where they'd take the young girls off
And dress them in a robe made
Of bear. A pelt to obscure
What men might see too soon and want,
Trained to grow their minds first.
The bear gave my girl a claw to tear beneath

The surface. Remember Red Rose's groom
Snagged to gold on the threshold?
This drift of the natural against her car
Gave her entry to the other land
Where tombs shine with fruit and flower.
Where babies' heads crown between
Animal legs. This bear came slowly for sacrifice
And so made holier the daughter I love
More than I love woods and words. Gave
Sacred to sacred. So I offer thanks.
It was as if I came out of the woods
To wake her with my great dull hand.

2.
Moving toward what I sensed, with my
Fourth-dimensional eye and ear,
My snout for rooting out beauty.
Like a bright berry in summer, though
It was dark. I could hear it coming.
Berry through the night, great circles
Of beauty and feast aimed at me.
And I left my mother's cave and my
Father's cave, for I was a bear
Grown to learn and I leathered
My way through trees to what
Was calling me. Like water
In a river the lights streamed.
I went to drink, thirsty, and the light
Smelled good. Keen to drink everything

On earth. The berry came quickly huge
And I met it with my head and mouth.
Paws in the air, I flew. The river
Slipped me back, and we both stalled.
Such stillness, the engine of the night
Beat in me. I was a bear receiving grace.
Gratitude to my ancestral tombs.
I was in the grail, ancient blood draining
The sound out of me. A human like
A white berry cried. I smelled
Fear and love. I'd never smelled
Love before in human form. Oh,
I'd known the rough jaw of my mother.
But human love came like a quail.
Something small and quick
Following its own kind. I inhaled
So I could make it last. I couldn't run.
I took to heart what metal sacrament
I had to take. Then I flew. Fled that smell
And river. Rose like Russian dancing bears,
Higher still. Saw that scene below
Smelling of tarmac and ponderosa pine.
Rising over a well-lit clump of humankind,
I donated my beauty to this girl. Sacrificed
My nudity and fur. I gave and gave
As the bullet fit my heart's cave.
I was the bear, and now she bore
My weight in her too small body
And I saw that she, of all of them,
Was one who understood and could.

Valentines for Soldiers

For the Gulf War

At the mission school in Española,
The children cut out hearts
And write messages of love.
My daughter, Hope, among them
Learning to cut and paste with urgency.

These days she cries more,
Follows me around after dark.
She goes back in time, fights more
With her brother, clings.
I think it's the war.

My older friend agrees.
Her children's children are the same,
And so is she, grandmotherly,
Yet uncertain how to grow
In this blitzed face of peace.

Their letters to the President didn't work.
No one listened to Hope's voice.
She sends valentines to soldiers,
Concentrates, pastes paper lace
Onto a red heart.

Velvet

I can't help screaming sometimes.
It's so soft the way children slipped into me;
The hard part comes with jaws and a clench like
Grasshoppers digesting what we've sown.

The corn, tender lettuces, arugula.
Nobody said arugula when I was young.
It's common knowledge daddy longlegs
Are the most venomous, but cannot bite.

I know only two things:
The antler of a deer has velvet
And a morning glory tendril
Yearns to twine and curl.

The things I know are soft.
The way my son opens his heart, the way
His hair felt after he cut five years' length,
Looking like the sixties in our house based on a sixties

Romance. My son hauls gravel in a green truck.
He's home only a week, but it's work we know him for
And work that keeps him strong. Like his father
And mine, his father's father.

And so we grew a man.
"Someday, he'll be helpful," the midwife said.
It was a full harvest moon. The house had no water.
His head was velvet.

Daughter in Summer

My daughter is a burden of flax.
Her hair, which is never combed
Is as fine as my patience.
Which is to say, tangled.

My daughter holding spit
In her mouth on the ride to Santa Fe
Breaks me in half like firewood
So I'll fit in her burners.

She has new teeth and a new
Ravishing nine-year-old face.
On roller blades
Her height is fast and streaming.

Under her comforter
She is level with me.
She smells our bed
With the day of her birth on it.

I am careful in loving, but not
Careful enough. Her face is mint
With four-sided stem. Her face
Is a plate of sunflowers.

In her body the engines of energy
Toil. Halfway between love and hate
I live with this summer child. Hating
Not her beauty, but my fractured fate.

My blood requires leeches. Prozac
And formaldehyde. Today failed me.
I praise her resilient blond head
That follows the sun of my maned face.

Tame hearts hold no interest for her
Though her mute smile might confuse you.
She misses no arrows. Catches lightning
And saves the lizard from the cat.

Holds the smallest chick in her hands
And keeps her hands cupped often
For the tenderness. I threw the I Ching
For my famished life. It gave me *Tenderness*,

What she was asking for. Small frogs.
Newborn guinea pigs. Anything to adore.
Her head resting next to her sister
And her sister's young man. The word, *mature*.

There is a young girl in the Española Valley
Who is alone except for a reading mother,
A telephone. The phone wire twists
Around the mother's legs all day.

At night the unwinding creates dust-devils
And the dogs bark. Out of the champagne air
Of Taos into the iris air of May, two of us
Locked into summer with keys to ninety days.

To my Teenage Son

It's not so impossible to love.
One thing leads to another heart.
You let birds fly in your window.
Remember the hummingbirds, how we'd catch
Them in baseball caps and set them free?
That's how hard it is to love.

It's like a snow day. One morning
The world is white, the radio's your friend,
And all day there's a warm drink, a sled,
Clothing comes on and off. Pour maple syrup
On snow and spoon up sweet blood of the tree.
Cold can be so cold it's hot.

You make eye contact with anyone.
It may lead to love. Love has destroyed
As much as it's created. This may scare you.
You, who prefer peaks of mountains, the whoop
Of your father's danger in your blood. Wild
Horse, guitar, music on loud for calculus.

The pleasure of good grades, love like that.
Love till it butters you, hurts. The reward is nothing
But pain pleasure pain. I can't show you love.
Your father loves me one way, without many words.
I love him wordily and loudly. I love him old
Since he was young.

You find your way. Leather jacket, watch,
Knife. That I love you doesn't help. Worst
Landscape for a son is mother-love. You are native
New Mexican, you informed us once. That alone
Puts you close to love, your ear on wind, your hand
On an ax. Your heart, an eye for beauty.

Part Three

✼

NO CURRENCY BUT LOVE

Coming back to the breath of love
When sometimes love was barely breathing.
Through the thick years and the thin,
Through the waist and ankles.
Coming back to the sky years,
The skeleton years, through
The think years and the thought.

Vexations

Fling aside all cares.
The lizard knows nothing peevish.
Arroyos only carry water
When water is there.

Violence gives me a headache.
I want my house wallpapered with flowers,
Not explosions and children's eyes,
Not rain forest lost to lumber lords.

Murder makes me uneasy in my armchair.
Midnight ticktocks, incendiary. I want laughter.
I want to cutup like the Marx Brothers.
This bothers me, my penchant for peace.

I knock on wood, kiss my mezuzah,
Cross fingers, pray. Mornings, I wake up
Optimistic like an olive branch
And never needing bifocals.

By night, the dark patterns terrorize.
No chair will hold me. Who can stand
In a holy place and not fear
For her life?

Miraculous Pantoum

I want to walk that rattlesnake walk,
Take off for anyplace that is not civil.
Let me invite you along, the weather's intense.
This is just someplace between miracles.

Take off, anyplace that is not civil,
Like Belize, Peru, or somewhere south and coastal.
This is just someplace between miracles,
Between Madonnas and stigmatas, a holiday of bikinis

Like Belize, Peru, or somewhere south and coastal.
Distance intrigues me because I'm stuck close at home,
Between Madonnas and stigmatas, a holiday of bikinis.
Among dish soaps, I hope to discover a new America,
     like Ferlinghetti.

I admire distances because the close scene at home
Grabs me by my female balls and zaps me.
Beyond dish soaps, I hope for a new America, like Ferlinghetti.
I'm ready to split like some sad beatnik with a past.

Grab me by my female balls and zap me.
I stand awake on my feet in the tracks of momma.
I'm ready to split like some sad beatnik with a history.
Let tomorrow come, lit like a ballpark for a night game.

I stand awake on my feet in the tracks of momma.
Let me invite you along, the weather's electric.
Let tomorrow come with its rattlesnake walk.
This is just someplace between miracles.

How to Improvise Rain

Take a shower and sing about rain.
Know that rain and grace are the same
Word in some Middle Eastern languages.

Say Grace, then water the lawn
With a Rain Bird sprinkler. Play Coltrane,
The Grateful Dead, or Ella Fitzgerald to your lawn.

Talk to the grass. Say, "La la la."
Pour dishwater on rosebushes.
Deconstruct the word *drought*.

Ought. Draft beer. Drama. Ouch.
Examine the sky for sky-looms, where rain
In the distance never hits the ground.

Make weather predictions.
Devise a theory about rain. Make life grainy
Through slow, long exposures.

Develop black-and-white
Film from a storm. Chant in Sanskrit
About the River Ganges.

Hand churn rain-flavored ice cream.
Wear ozone perfume. Play a kettledrum
Softly. Do not waste tears.

But cry. Go to sad movies. Find a man
Who cries. Marry for moisture not money.
Make love on a roof. Have wet children.

Go to the Rainbow Dance at Santa Clara and love
Children holding painted rainbows in their hands.
Watch the backdrop of clouds darken, wince at lightning.

Buy a pass to the local pool. Hang laundry,
Wash a car as sacrifice. Put on white slacks and walk
Along Paseo de Peralta. Improvise grace.

Save bathwater and send it to the apple.
Learn a song in the Tewa language.
Dance till you sweat to "The River of Babylon."

Petition Saint Jude.
Read these words outside.
Name your son Noah.

Ghost Town

No one vacuums in a far-off town
Where the wind devils the house.
No clothes flap on the lines, their wings
And nobody bothers dust.

I go to a town where no one lives.
They have these places in the West.
In Pennsylvania everything is filled,
Time with work, parlors with chairs.

Houses demand to be cleaned,
Babies to be fed. Back home, women daydream
About the West. New Mexico is empty,
Lures dreamers.

Here I daydream all the time
About a ghost house full of wind.
All the windows gone and the songs
Come through, honky-tonk and blues.

They all start alone and end there.
They all grab me up, but when the wind
Sets me down I'm home, a cluttered room,
A phone, a collection of rocks and bone.

I'm back in the family I was born for,
Not the one I came from.

This Time

When I met my teacher
This time, walking through woods,
I wasn't hungry like a wolf,
Famished, or a ghost.
I was thirsty but didn't know it,
As in winter. I drank
The way clay takes water,
Slaked even by mist.

When I met my beloved this time,
On the street of my favorite city,
I wasn't greedy. One vowel
Gave me the whole story.
One taste was a banquet.
The eyelash that fell on his cheek
Was a body of pleasure.
His glance held history,
The future, and now.

When I met my mother
This time, in the middle
Of my large life, I didn't want
To shrink and climb back inside her.
I wanted to wave banners that said,
Bon Voyage. Fly prayer flags
And toast, *L'Chaim*, for the life
She gave me.

When I met my children
On the road, whizzing by,
This time, I brushed the spiderwebs
Of guilt aside and said, "Pedal hard.
You'll arrive on time. Take long rests
To drink, watch birds, the warbler,
The crow, to know that thing earned."

When I saw my Holy One
This time, everlasting November,
We held the full world trembling
In a cup. We both drank it,
A cup of nightfall, a cup of planets,
A cup of pasture, a cup of honey,
A cup of stillness, a cup of journey,
A cup full of roses.

Reminiscence about the Present

You are sleeping, your heart
From God's country, being my
Valentine in sleep.

The poems about our marriage make
Our marriage, as much as money does,
As much as food.

February 14, 1995. Remember that morning
You asked to sleep in, at least
Till work time? A Thursday.

Like the day Vallejo died in Paris,
Like all the Thursdays of long life.
But this specific Thursday so becalmed

The clouds darkening the mountains,
Making up for an open winter.
Valentines of clouds not chocolate,

Valentines of dogs, not roses. A lifetime
Of accumulated kisses, like snow
More than comestibles, like mud

As much as sentiment. I loved it that day,
Right now, when we were young
As we'll ever be, near fifty.

I remember how it was
Now, when I practiced
Loving you forever.

Making Ends Meet

Simply because you love me
And always forgive, I advise all women
To marry. It's lousy advice.
It's free from my gusty mouth.

Simply because I gave you all my years
And am always having children
My days stay sane as Sunday, as
Rocks in their place, as mustard bloom.

Making ends meet. My dog once chased
His tail. These days go round. The baby
Has the croup, makes the hollow sound
Of geese, of cities when you're alone.

I come home late. You're upstairs.
The lights all on. Spaghetti
Grows bigger in its pot of cool water.
I tiptoe in on your sleep

And find you curled around the baby
Simply because you love.
You give me air and wood
And I catch on fire.

Finishing Touches

After a fight
A man and woman turn to activity.
He is shining his cordovan shoes.
With a sock and paste from a tin
Adorned by a wingless bird.

She uses polish with a childhood smell
To remove tarnish from an antique
Silver nutmeg grater
He stole for her from his aunt.

What she really wants
Is to polish his face
With her kiss
And restore its grace.

What he wants, as he pulls
The tongue out of the shoe,
Is for her harsh voice to sweeten
Back to when both of them were new.

Simplicity

Do you like simplicity
Or do you have a secret desire to be stirred?
I wish I could borrow Rumi's body
And feel what longing felt like in the thirteenth century.

Do you have a desire for being stirred?
Are you modern or classical, contemporary?
Feel what longing felt like in the thirteenth century.
Charles Olson said, "Style is soul."

Are you modern or classical, contemporary,
Or do you revere Jesus, birth to resurrection?
Charles Olson said, "Style is soul."
Jesus died to save our style.

Do you revere Jesus, birth to resurrection?
The shrines and churches move me, where
Jesus died to save our style.
At Chimayo the candles heat sincerely.

The shrines and churches move me, where
Votives burn to hail Mary, requiems for sinners.
At Chimayo the candles heat sincerely.
I am not Catholic. My heart's non-denominational.

Votives burn to hail Mary, requiems for saints.
I wear crosses for the four directions.
I am not Catholic. My heart's non-denominational.
My daughters and I dance to rap, reggae, and soul.

I wear crosses to the four directions.
I wish I could borrow Rumi's body,
Dance to reggae, rap, and soul.
Or, do you prefer simplicity?

The New Field

Out beyond ideas of right doing
And wrong doing there is a field.
I'll meet you there.
—RUMI

If Shams of Tabriz, Rumi's beloved, arrives
In the form of a young woman, it is I who begin to

Whirl. Shams did arrive, spinning this marriage
Into gold. Translating ashes into horses.

I who was married to no one in the city
Of lost causes shook my dull head *yes!*

Though I was terrified, with death nipping
At my heels, my heart enlivens.

I ask you to prepare the garden soil.
Enlightenment needs good dirt, plenty

Of shit, fresh green turned under and blue
Eyes of amazing women, brown eyes of men

Living and men dead. All are assembling
In your heart. I'll meet you there.

Speaking of Happiness

I want you to be happy
So I look to the rain.
Lotus grow on the lake
On the way to the Pure Land.
Maybe you'll never be content
This side of death. Paradise
Is a walled garden. You don't believe
In walls, though a good fight
And a barbed-wire fence will do.
When rain falls through, no snags.

I watered all the plants
With rainwater, trying to soften
The life we've aged. I look at
What gravity taught you last fall
Hunting elk at Santa Barbara, saint
Of fire. Riding out alone with our horses
Blanco and Dollar Bill. Two.
And you. Gravity calling
The rain and the elk calling
Each other for love at night.

It is sweet to smell you back
From the hunt. The rain all night
Though we were estranged,
Rang a perfect tone. Childhood
Farm rain, city rain. Unborn
Rain. Duty and commerce gone.
Time to milk cows for rain,
Time to harvest bread-and-butter
Corn. Time to be happy, this side
Of the grave. Where gravity
Told you all about love.

Another Fiesta

At dawn we walked miles to watch color,
Breath and frill of hot-air balloon fiesta.
Finally drove home, northerly or southerly,
It is this homing we adore.

You explain the elk hunt. Gravity
Became your teacher, your pact.
You considered gravity from horseback
From beside a stream, by fire, inside a tent.

You are driving seventy five, talking
With your hands. Our daughter sleeps.
You tell me gravity is love.
The water never leaves the ocean

Because the earth loves it.
I move my hand onto yours.
I have always been a grave woman.
I think you're telling why you love me.

But you are speaking about the rivers,
How the elk bugle in the night, gone
By morning. How happy you were, alone.
This moment, before we reach home

Credits and debits flowering in a rural
Mailbox, before our daughter wakes,
I think, how lucky that when I was ten
And you were twelve I asked at school,

"Why doesn't the water fall out of
The ocean?" and the entire class shouted
"Gravity!" at me, like a curse.
How lucky, that you would answer me now

When I would be so ready to listen.
When I would be so heavily pleased.

Qualicum

(Place where the big fish pass)
Qualicum Beach, B.C, 1996

I gave him a flower
From Qualicum
And by the end of the hour
We had crushed it, crushed
It, we had torn all the purple
From the stalk.

I brought him the flower
With a name I hadn't learned,
I was only loaned its fragrance and shape
Which was exactly his shape
In a certain slant and mood.

As on this morning, after
The sun rose inside my old chest
And "Las Mañanitas" played me back
To New Mexico. Tears for departure,
We'll linger here, let the ferry go
And catch a later one
Crossing to Horseshoe Bay.

I brought him an unnamed flower
So he loved me back to India
And the story of Ganesh, who moves
The unmovable across three continents,
Through time zones and two thousand years
Where temple walls are carved
With voluptuous embrace, and Shiva
And Shakti speak in whispered syllables.
There are other lifetimes at stake.

We, old lovers too, carve a fragile frieze
Into momentary sheets. Our blessed limbs
And hearts will not be chronicled here.
Can only be sung in the days
Before the Vedas were written down
By the elephant with four arms,
Connoisseur of sweets, remover
Of obstacles, who gave me a flower
From a tree on the boulevard

Outside our rented room, highway thick
With truck sounds that we used
To hide our own sounds at the Sunset
Inn at Qualicum this morning.

Leaving Seattle

I invite us back to the ocean, anytime,
Where we were meant to rinse in phosphorescence
At night, our skins the stuff of constellations.

We have learned to be tidal together,
Eat Pin Cove clams, breathe as the moon breathes.
The world we exhale into grows alive.

A street singer sings us, "Cupid, lend me
Your bow." And the next street singer too.
In the celadon days of Seattle we found our song,

And the Pacific fed us oysters in little tantric
Bites. We met as if by chance
After twenty-five years of close company.

After Our Silver Anniversary

Third night in our own bed
Finally the rains flatter the new
Red roof. You tap me like we tap
Maple for its rising blood.

You find your sweet way home.
Lightning visits our room.
The bell of night rings.
Red rain soothes our red roof.

Vajra to meditate upon
During my first childbirth
And by my third I was looking out at clouds,
Quoting Mirabai, "Without the energy

That moves mountains, how am I to live?"
In the middle of love my friend
Who is dying lies down in my mind.
What we do is the prayer for him.

As we both let go, rebirth, miracle,
Resurrection, all manner of impossible
Acts in this simple bed where our child
Was made and born. We grow terrible

With love, and the rain
After so much drought,
Smothers doubt, too. Thunder,
A pillow to muffle our noise.

We have heard God's voice only
In privacy. We make time. Then
A few words. What are words
When we live so briefly in bodies?

What are bodies but ground
For the birth of hearts?
We come home to love and make
Sacred forms older than temples.

I Thought it was My Heart

But it was the tent selling fireworks in Tesuque.
It glowed a week before the Forth of July
With its celebratory gusto. My heart's zeal
Was sealed in amber, tree from that long ago.

I thought it was my heart, but it was your voice
On the answering machine, my only son
Living in another state, finding out what voice
Comes from loneliness and what from family
And what voice trees and landscape make.

I thought it was my other heart, but it was you
Lying in a hotel after a meeting, that body
We have shared at feast and famine suns
Itself in solitude, and I thought it was mine
Always, before meeting and after death,
But it was a life lived separate from my longing.

I thought it was my best heart, but it was my daughter
Her face in silver of photography, with a profile
Better than the mountains because I saw it first,
Loved it, sang to it, the private delicacy
Of first child to woman meant to be a mother.

I thought it was my last heart, but it was you,
Poised at the computer screen, all day
While I lazed and hung laundry, dreamed and
Used the telephone for love and business,
Hunted for my soul and found you, small handed
And perfect. Only ten, but with a perfect number
Of ideas and a perfect future almost living itself
Right now. And I thought it was my heart.

Late Vows

I'd like to marry you again,
Not with ceremony, but with distance
As trees grow rougher with age.

I'm not so old, but tougher now myself.
I'm silhouette, I'm shadow. Turn to me,
If you don't want me, exit, I'll exist.

There are a thousand cranes,
Ten thousand cities in the world,
But few things I want. You are one.

If this suits you, fine.
If it doesn't, fine also, I love
The taste of tears, they are another tea

That feeds. My gift before was pain,
I long for passion now, open to expanse.
Are you willing to age beside me?

It won't be easy, this I promise.
I vow nothing, a cracked heart, a bed,
But I only want you. Join me in our solitudes.

Gesticulations

If I grow older and lose all memory,
Having no more dates and only names that serve,
If you are beside me, I will put my hand
In your back pocket. Blue jeans never age.
My hand alive against you.

If I have no hands, I will place my heart
Under your hat. I will smell your hair
With my reliable heart, and love how colorless
Your hair smells. I can tell we haven't grown wise.
We'll fight our fabulous fights

Grown fuller and fuller of laughter. The same
Fights fought so long they'll be choreographed.
A stiff old Russian ballet with many leaps.
You will be kissing my Bolshoi hem and I
Will curtsy in the next millennium.

If I have no heart, I will bite into your arm.
I will follow by my teeth, leaving curved marks.
And I'll taste how your arm has done so much for me,
Carried things in from the trunk, brought me to pleasure
And pain, built the house, swaddled the child.

If I'm toothless and vision gone,
If I am bodiless, if I'm dead before you,
I will still be a gesture in our daughter's shoulder.
She will shrug and it will be my indifference.
She'll smile, I'll be flashing semaphore.

This rehearsal of loss so I can feel the life
We actually are. Not the taxes we pay
On the love we've cashed, but anxious holy love
Driving over the washboard road. We've scrubbed
Each other clean, rubbed each other right and wrong.

It is finally sinking in, total recall,
These gestures of thick and thin, once and for all.

Blessing

Dear my heart
Maker of mitzvahs on my body,
All the earth fills with our blessings
Angels surround us for Shabbos.
Holy one of patience and good will,
Not even God comes as close to me
Though you give me tastes of God.
Blessing of the husband, blessing
Of the wife. The whole night wine,
And braided and light.

✒ *Gratitudes* ✒

To my ever-darling Judyth Hill who read this manuscript with me, helped me figure out my entire year, and left chocolates and poetry on the pillow. To Renée Gregorio, for trading manuscripts and her editorial sense that is attuned to the muse. To my Michael, for his wild exuberance, horses, computer patience, and other strains of patience. To Joe Mowrey, for urging me to take this manuscript out of chaos and into completion. To Rabbi Chavah Carp for teaching me about blessed resistance from its biblical origins at Creation itself.

✒ *About the Author* ✒

Joan Logghe has been an integral part of New Mexico's poetry renaissance for many years. She has appeared as a workshop leader, keynote speaker, or reader in a variety of settings, locally and nationally, including Armand Hammer United World College, the Taos Institute, Vancouver International Writer's Festival, and Ghost Ranch at Abiquiu New Mexico. She is winner of a National Endowment in Poetry, a Barbara Deming Memorial/Money for Women grant, and the Language of Life contest on KNME TV for her poem, "Something Like Marriage." She is presently on the Speaker's Bureau for the New Mexico Endowment for the Humanities.

Logghe is founder and director of Write Action: Writing from the Heart of AIDS, a grassroots organization which brings free writing workshops to Santa Fe's AIDS community and others facing illness, trauma, or loss. She presents writing and literature as a bridge to emotional activism.

Books include, *Twenty Years in Bed with the Same Man* (La Alameda Press), *Sofia* (La Alameda Press), *Catch Our Breath: Writing from the Heart of AIDS* (Mariposa Printing & Publishing), and *Another Desert: Jewish Poetry of New Mexico* (Sherman Asher Press) edited with Miriam Sagan.

She and her husband live in La Puebla, New Mexico where they built a solar home and are joined by a cast of three children, two horses, and chickens too numerous to mention here by name.